Graphic Design For Beginners

Secrets To Graphic Design Revealed!

By: Jason Scotts

TABLE OF CONTENTS

Publishers Notes.. 3

Dedication 4

Chapter 1- Why Study Graphic Design 5

Chapter 2- The Work Of Graphic Designers....................... 8

Chapter 3- How To Become A Graphic Designer.............. 12

Chapter 4- Degree or Without Degree?.............................. 15

Chapter 5- Graphic Design Programs 18

Chapter 6- Choosing A Graphic Design School................. 21

Last Words 25

About The Author...28

PUBLISHERS NOTES

DEDICATION

This book is dedicated to aspiring digital artists, graphics artists and our mentors.

CHAPTER 1- WHY STUDY GRAPHIC DESIGN

Your interest is certainly caught by the many graphic images and designs in different advertisements in print, television and the Internet. You may notice that all products are coming up with the best and most attention catching designs and visuals to help attract the attention of people, particularly of prospective consumers.

If you ever wonder about the talents that made the visually appealing materials, then you must brace yourself to get to know the world of graphics designers. Graphics designers are the creative experts behind all the ads and visual plugs being posted in print, billboard, television and the Internet. The person is responsible for the interesting images on pictures or moving graphics in videos.

In the past, graphics designers' works rely heavily on creativity. But because times have changed, graphics designers are now provided with many graphic aids and tools. However, graphic designers can either consider those as a boon or as a bane.

Modern computer software and tools are spread out across the market to help complement the talents, skills and creativity of graphics designers. However, because of the significant number of those aids, the graphic designers are now confused on which to choose. Different graphic designing tools are also taking edges over each other. Thus, a graphic designer may be at a dilemma because a software may contain features he needs, while the other services can be found at another graphic designing program.

If you aim to be a graphics designer in the future, you would need to remember that it is graphics designers' responsibility to present information and content in ways that would be accessible and at the same time very much appealing to the public. Graphics designers usually produce designs to promote clients' products and services. The world of advertising is really competitive, so graphic designs must always be more appealing if not as effective as the currently rolled out.

The demanding taste and preference of the viewing public is also a cause of concern for graphics designers. These creative experts must know the target audience and must determine which strategies and styles would best work for the intended public. Thus, graphics designers are advised to earn diplomas or degrees from academic institutions and learning centers that are known to produce experts for such job tasks.

Just like journalists, graphics designers are also advised to develop through time their own working and output portfolio. Such compiled materials would highlight the talent and creative capacity. Potential clients and employers usually check out such portfolios to initially gauge the skills and expertise of a graphic designer.

Portfolios of modern graphic designers are now also modernized. The sophistication of computer graphics must be reflected on the outputs so that prospective clients would determine the level of expertise, reliability and creativity of graphic designers.

Portfolios can be formatted digitally so that immediate access can be provided to those needing to check the outputs out. In the past, previous graphic designs must be compiled in black books and binders. Now, everything can be stored digitally and electronically so that retrieval would be easily facilitated as long as there is access to computers, particularly to the Internet.

Such a portfolio system is a demonstration of how graphic designers can take advantage of the modern and sophisticated tools available through computer and online media. There is also a clearer and easier point of comparison.

Businesses, particularly advertisers, are in constant need of graphic designers. While in the past, companies needed skilled workers, now, graphic designers are necessities because they do the tasks of effectively conveying to customers messages and contents necessary for different business transactions.

The world of marketing, advertising and plain businesses would never do without graphic designers. Thus, such workers are deemed as among the most important professionals across all industries. If you aim to become one, you surely would realize that there are far greater opportunities for earning..

Chapter 2- The Work Of Graphic Designers

Basically, the role of each graphic designer is to facilitate a productive and creative flow of communication. The conveyance process can be one-way, when the company conveys an important message to target audience, and two-way, when the graphics designer is commissioned to facilitate a flow of communication when the target audience is given the ability and means to react or provide feedback regarding the conveyed message.

The graphics designer is usually hired by companies to get involved in the planning, analyzing and of course, designing of a visual communication strategy. That way, the graphics designer is left to strategize on how the important message can be conveyed using media like print, motion picture and of course, the popular electronic or online portals. The methodology of having the message sent across could be in the form of animation, photography, illustrations, text content and many more.

In the modern corporate scene, the basic roles of graphic designers are as follows:

- Layouting print materials like newspapers, corporate brochures, magazines, reports and journals. Graphic designers are also commissioned to design visually appealing presentations. Other materials designed and produced by these professionals are marketing brochures, promotional displays and logos and packaging of services and products.

- Film graphic designers are responsible for producing the credits seen at the beginning and at the end of motion pictures, television shows or any video presentation.
- Graphic designers are employed to enliven content. Illustrations in books and other printed and published materials are principally outputs of these experts.

- The computer and creative graphics in television shows and videos, like video captions and weather forecast maps and illustrations, are domains of graphic designers.

- Design and layout of Web pages across the online media are responsibilities of graphic designers. Thus, these materials are almost always visually appealing. Studies have shown that overall perception and reception of online users are influenced by how Web pages appear. Visually appealing ones are almost always well patronized and often visited by guests.

Thus, it can easily be inferred that there is a wide array of opportunities posed to the modern graphic designers. There are too many avenues for creativity and productivity that could be taken by such highly competent professionals.

However, the graphics designer is also expected to develop an inner talent in knowing what the target audience would prefer and choose. Creative outputs would render futile if they are not properly and appropriately targeted to intended audience. And so like most communicators, graphics designers must get a grip of what would appeal and catch attention of prospective clients.

When designing and developing products and services for clients, graphics designers principally take into consideration the cognitive, social, physical and cultural factors. Coordination must be established between them and their paying clients do that intended results and goals could be definitely set. When needed, graphics designers must also know how to conduct basic researches to make the proposed outputs even more effective.

Graphic designers must know the audience, first and foremost. As much as possible basic demographics and characteristics of the target audience must be put into consideration so that final outputs would surely be effective. Failure to establish that knowledge would almost always put the efforts to futility. Ideas not properly and effectively communicated would be put to waste, equating to higher non-productive expenses for the client companies.

As a graphics producer, designers are logically and naturally expected to integrate different elements like artwork, photography, colors, animation, graphs or charts and even sounds into their outputs. And they should do this integration in a fashion that would obviously and naturally be recognized and appreciated by intended audience.

Moreover, graphics designers and copywriters are estranged bed partners because they must always work with one another to complement each other. Both would be able to produce and develop their best products through collaboration and coordination.

On top of all these, graphic designers are expected to be knowledgeable in every important software needed to make their outputs more appealing, visually stimulating and effective. It is part of their human capital and investment to get accustomed and exposed to such necessities so that their natural talents and creativity would be further enhanced. However, it is still very basic that graphics designers know the general and very conventional knowledge and skills of using the old or traditional methods of producing creative outputs.

CHAPTER 3- HOW TO BECOME A GRAPHIC DESIGNER

For every profession, of course, there are qualifications that are set to determine and justify a person's competence to do the required tasks. Most companies hiring graphics designers want to tap applicants who are very knowledgeable and are highly reliable on all the technical aspects pertinent to the graphics-designing job.

Most companies require graphics designers to own a Bachelor's degree to make sure they would be fit and competent to deliver what are required by the job. If not a Bachelor's degree, the graphics designers are required to have at least an Associate degree.

The basic college degree especially designed to provide basic training and knowledge for graphics designers is Bachelor's of Fine Arts. Such degree programs are currently being offered at major universities and colleges around the world. There are public as well as private academic institutions that are offering such degree programs.

Included courses in the degree programs are design principles, studio art, computer designing, printing techniques, commercial graphics and Web site designing. Like most Bachelor's degrees, Fine Arts usually are accompanied by general electives like psychology, liberal arts, writing, art history, cultural studies, sociology, marketing and foreign languages. All these courses are proven to be helpful in broadening the perspective of graphic designers so that they would be more knowledgeable about other pertinent subjects that can be potentially useful in designs.

Associate degrees and basic certificates for graphics designing are providing trainees and students with the just the basics in the tasks. Usually, such programs are taken within two to three years.

Many design schools and centers are operating at major cities all over the world to help produce and supply designers to the ever growing industries.

Such minor degrees and diplomas are normally tackling just the basic and technical aspects of graphic designing. Many graphic designers are holding these degrees because they are more time efficient and are less costly to acquire. Plus, many companies recognize the effectiveness and reliability of the knowledge and skills rendered by such designers.

If you are already a degree holder in another discipline, it is still not too late for you. You could easily pursue a budding career in graphics designing by taking additional subjects or courses that are basic to the practice. You must attain the basic knowledge and skills to do the tasks required by clients.

Aside from these degrees, graphic designers are expected to be highly proficient in using the modern and sophisticated computer tools for layouting and graphic designing. Employers always assume that graphic designers are experts in computer graphics designing, on top of skills on conventional graphics designing.

Because computers are regularly updating and there are numerous software for graphics designing, graphic designers need to be constantly updated about the latest technology in computer aids. Such professionals must always be adept with the latest software packages that should be used in making the outputs better and more effective.

On top of all those skills and expertise, the graphics designers first and foremost, must have inborn and genuine creativity. They must be artful and must be experts in producing art pieces no matter what media and tools are used. Creativity is an inborn talent and is developed over time or since birth. Therefore, not all willing to be graphics designers would be effective in pursuing such careers. Creativity for some is a God-given talent; some will be oozing with it while others simply are not blessed with them.

After all the above qualifications are met, the graphics designers would again be subjected to a period of training by their respective companies so that these professionals would be oriented and made more adept at the basics and demands of the profession. On the job trainings also make graphics designers attuned with the requirements and the consistent style maintained by companies. You see, firms have trademark designs and design characteristics that are almost always made unique to them.

Moreover, basic interest and passion would be a key to success. As always, sheer talent and skills would not be enough if the professional would not have enough determination and motivation to make things work as intended. Proper attitude and working ethics are also needed as those features would help make the graphics designer be totally effective and reliable.

CHAPTER 4- DEGREE OR WITHOUT DEGREE?

As people all know, owning a corresponding degree is very much essential for professionals. Generally undergraduate and graduate degrees are considered passports to a profession. For example, doctors must take the necessary and required degrees to be able to practice their profession. In the case of graphics designers, a degree in graphics designing is imperative so that potential employers would be assured that the person is really qualified and adequately skilled for the profession.

Almost all companies require applicants for the graphics designing position to present evidences that they are holding appropriate Bachelor's or Associate degrees. That is because such firms want to make sure the applicant would be good enough and would be highly reliable to render the tough job that would be asked from them.

High school students and young people aiming to enter the industry of graphics designing should be reminded that they should spend a significant amount of time and efforts in taking appropriate and recommended degrees for the job. There are numerous private and public universities all over the world that are focusing and are making good at offering degrees and courses for graphics designing.

Degrees from good and highly credible graphics design schools, colleges and universities are proven to help develop and mold good graphics designers. To begin with, there are theories and academic principles that are designed to help beginners and new entrants to graphics designing. The basic academic electives can also be helpful in making sure the student would be well adept and knowledgeable about other factors and subjects that can be of great help in graphics designing.

There are still many people who argue about the need for basic degrees in graphics designing. Obviously, these people are those who do not possess enough and appropriate Bachelor's or Associate degrees for them to fully practice in the profession. These people insist that common people would always learn to get on to the job if they are only creative and talented enough.

Truthfully, such arguments make sense. But through history, experts and industry practitioners would insist that the best graphics designers are those who own appropriate and rightful degrees to practice the profession. To conservationists, there are just too much basic knowledge imparted by degrees and courses in college that can be helpful to the practice.

For example, history of art can be of great help for any aspiring graphics designer. That is because through the subject, the student would be exposed to the past contemporary arts. Having that exposure can help any student modify his artistic style. If there would be any designs using the past and ancient arts, the graphics designer would also likely not encounter problems.

While others would still argue that real talent, creativity and plain interest in graphics deigning is all that matter, professionals would assert that lack of formal and proper discipline and training would prevent anyone from getting into the industry. Most practitioners very well know that it would take more before anyone can be recognized as a bonafide and real graphics designer.

Should graphics designers be degree holders? The answer is a resounding yes. During these times when competition is really tough and job demands are really intense, it would significantly help if the graphics designers would be able to provide all the required documents and credentials. Talent is not enough, as many would say. Currently, there should something to be added to talent. And that is sheer college degrees.

As a matter of fact, most companies all around the world would always require college degrees when entertaining job applications. For those firms, owning college degrees would be an effective and sure assurance that graphics designers would be highly creative, competent and very much skilled.

If you are aiming to become a good and reliable graphics designer, what are you waiting for? Move and initiate to earn the necessary degree you ought to take. Finding such offering at major universities would surely be not hard.

Currently, graphics designers are one of the most in demand professionals all around the world. The law of supply and demand states that when the supply is scarce, prices would rise. In the real world of graphics designing, the constantly rising demand for graphic artists is very promising because that means companies would compete to lure applicants and new graduates though higher compensation.

CHAPTER 5- GRAPHIC DESIGN PROGRAMS

Almost all popular and successful graphics designers nowadays have one thing in common: all of them are degree holders. Though arguments are still lurking about whether earning such degrees are imperative in the practice, companies are still widely honoring the belief that proper courses and programs would help make a good and reliable graphics designer.

Degrees are basically considered passports to practicing graphics designing. Without proper college and associate degrees advertising and marketing firms would not provide opportunities even for the most talented graphics makers. That is because modern working environments recognize the importance of attaining other useful knowledge. Workers who are all around are more reliable, smarter and are proven to be more productive in the long run because they would always use their broad knowledge base to whatever endeavor they take.

For graphics designers, it would be helpful if they would also hold relevant exposure to copywriting. Though they need not be expert writers, it would be useful if they would have the skill to at least have skills in basic editing and proper usage. Graphics designers are meant to work with copywriters but there are instances when they have to rely on their own personal convictions and knowledge about grammar.

Owning a Bachelor's degree is also a guarantee that the graphics designer has the right amount of discipline to get things going. In college, students are trained to be hard working and resourceful. It is assumed that being fully adjusted to the tedious and hectic college life, professionals would easily cope up with the normal casual office environment.

If a Bachelor's degree is too weighty, aspiring graphics designers could opt to take an Associate degree instead. Bachelor's degree is on the average about four years to fully complete. On the other hand, Associate degrees are usually taken within about two to three years. Such programs also make sure that the courses taken by students are only those necessary to basic computer or systems graphics designing.

Aside from the two basic graphics designing degrees, there are also minor programs for everyone. For professionals who already own degrees but not related to graphics designing, they could opt to enlist in diploma programs. Such programs are shorter in scope and time frame from the Associate degrees. Taking certificates in graphics designing is the easiest because the student is only provided with the really less and lean data and subjects.

If you aim to be a good graphics designer, you should start by having proper ambition. No matter how hard the ladder would get, be sure to step up in it slowly but surely. Graphics designers are professionals and by such, are almost always the relevant degrees for the job.

Finding the learning center to earn such degrees is also not hard. You would realize that those courses and programs are almost always offered in the major and gigantic public and universities in almost all countries. Thus, each country has its own set of universities that are known to take much of the productive and very creative produce.

When you aim to attain graphics designing degrees or certificates, all you need to do is to enlist in the right school and prepare financially for the endeavor. You would surely notice that graphics designers are very resourceful. They are almost always able to rise from their troubles. That can be an effect of graduating from the most prestigious and known companies across all countries.

When you get to study in such universities, you would find that you could make use of your assets and talents enormously. Being resourceful means that most students would always have something to do about certain challenges. That is college life. Every student would be exposed on how life really and actually goes.

If you are out to earn the necessary degree for you to be able to become a graphics designer, you should first seek to open yourself to learn about a lot of things. You should take usual and knowledge-packed courses and electives so that your perspective and knowledge base would be broadened for your own good.

CHAPTER 6- CHOOSING A GRAPHIC DESIGN SCHOOL

Before moving to take a degree for graphics designing, it is imperative that you first settle to make a wise and sound decision on which school or academic institution you would be going to earn your credentials. As mentioned in the previous chapters, owning a Bachelor's or an Associate's degree is necessary before anyone can penetrate into the graphics designing industry.

With hundreds of institutions and academic centers focusing on providing quality education, students are almost always in dilemmas in choosing the right and appropriate university for them. All around the world, there are numerous universities that have been training students to the basics of graphics designing.

In most global cities, there are computer schools that are starting to focus on programs that are specifically for computer graphics designing. Even state and private universities are offering courses and programs that are essential for becoming graphics designers.

If you are aiming to earn a degree program that is basic and necessary for graphics designing, it would be helpful if you would first seek expert and public opinion about the academic institution. It is important to make sure the education center is very much credible and is reliable in providing good and quality education. Future employers would certainly take particular attention to where the degree of the graphics-designing applicant is coming from.

To be able to gauge the credibility and competence of a university in providing the best possible education, it is important to take note of the quality of graduates produced. Observe the market and find information about the universities where professionals earned their degrees. Graduates are the best testimonials and proofs of the quality of education provided by an academic institution.

The next factor to consider when finding the right school to earn a graphics designing degree would be the overall standing of the university. Every year, there are polls and indexes that are aiming to gauge the effectiveness and quality of global universities. From those lists, you would easily find the best schools in the country where you are coming from.

Recommendations from peers and experts would also be essential. If there are such professionals who are offering advice as to where students could best attain degrees. It would be effective if students would take the heed and enroll in such endorsed universities.

Looking at the course outline and the curriculum would also be helpful when deciding which university to attend. To be able to choose the best school to attain the graphics designing degree, it would be important if you would first look at the program and determine if the courses and subjects included would be essential and helpful to make you become a qualified and effective graphics designer in the future. If there are numerous courses that are not too important, it would be wise to find another institution.

Looking at the tuition fees would also give you hint as to how good a university is. Of course, state colleges have lower fees because the programs offered are all subsidized by the government. Expensive schools are almost always assuring quality of education. That is because those costly schools allocate a significant portion of the fees to improving facilities and hiring the best and qualified instructors and professors.

There are also distance education centers that are offering such programs. Many people are now starting to realize the importance of earning degrees at the comfort of home. Convenience is very much characterized by such programs. When you decide to take degrees from distance education centers, you would be able to do other things, like taking part time jobs or attending other schools. Be reminded that such settings are also more pressuring on your part because you would be left to learn on your own using the modules to be provided by the school.

After you initially chose which institution to go to, you would then proceed to consider the following. You should take note of the entrance and enrolment requirements. Usually, entrance tests and screening are conducted so those universities would gauge the competence and knowledge of the future students. In state universities, you would almost always compete for the slot. You would be surprised that there are numerous students aiming to enter state universities. Thus, the competition is more intense.

Also take a look at the academic requirements and at the system of grading. If you are not comfortable with the learning system implemented in the university, find another one. Universities would not modify their tried and tested systems just to accommodate you.

Schools that are known to have ties and partnerships with industry players are recommendable. Usually, students would aim to attend college in such universities because they would be assured that once they completed the program, they would have greater chances at being included in the industry's most reliable and popular graphics designing teams.

LAST WORDS

It is estimated that in the United States alone, about 40% of the total designing employees across all industries are made up of graphics designers. There are numerous advertising and marketing firms that are mostly composed of talented and skilled graphics designers. Thus, it is clear that the demand for such professionals all over the world is imminently rising.

Through the years, many companies have been relying on the quality of services and products being produced by good graphics designers. Sales and popularity of products and companies are very much dependent on the effectiveness of the graphics designs provided by professionals.

Thus, there are many students who are aiming to take necessary and required credentials and degrees for graphics designing. However, be reminded that necessary degrees are not enough to make sure you would pass as a qualified and really effective graphics designer. Sheer creativity and right attitude are also significant and important factors that would help ensure your success.

Creativity is never acquired. It is an inborn quality that is inept in all of us. The levels of creativity, however, varies because people deal with the characteristic differently. Those who cultivated and nourished creativity early in life are tending to become more graphical and visual.

Technology is also one factor that redefines the graphics designing industry. In the past, graphics designers were relying on their talent to draw and make good and interesting products through their artistic sides. Now, computer skills are more essential. There are numerous computer software that have been developed to provide graphics designers with right tools and aids for making their projects work. Graphics designers need to be adept and experts in using such computer programs.

Graphics designers must also learn how to work with a team. Usually, communication campaigns and projects are not carried out by graphics designers alone. There must be copywriters and researchers in such teams. That is to make sure the creative and visually appealing presentation would be complemented by good content. Best designed ads and visuals coming with the best contents possible would surely make a project really effective.

The purpose of graphics designing is to make sure communication strategies would be as effective as possible. In the corporate scene, companies produce visuals and ads to convince people to patronize products and services. The mode of communication is almost always persuasive in nature. Thus, graphics designers must be skilled and adept in making designs that would not just call attention of intended audience, but also make them instantly ready to make the call of action.

If you aim to be a graphics designer in the future, you would need to remember that it is graphics designers' responsibility to present information and content in ways that would be accessible and at the same time very much appealing to the public. Graphics designers usually produce designs to promote clients' products and services. The world of advertising is really competitive, so graphic designs must always be more appealing if not as effective as the currently rolled out.

Thus, you must have the proper and recommended credentials and skills. Earning such credentials is not hard. You need to be determined and open minded in finding the best possible institutions where you would attain Bachelor's or Associate degrees. There are so many schools all over the world, but only a few are known to produce quality and best graduates.

The Internet has redefined how graphics designers work. Now, visuals are mostly focused at being posted at Web sites. Almost all people are now taking access to the online media. Thus, companies aim to boost their Internet presence. Internet initiatives currently make up the bulk of regular and usual jobs and tasks performed by qualified graphics designers.

Thus, to become a good graphics designer, you need to be exposed to the modes and nature of Internet publishing. There are numerous competing sites online, so it would be the graphics designers' challenge to make sure the Web site is as good if not way better than the rest.

If you aim to be a good graphics designer, be patient, be creative, be open to new ideas and be receptive to knowing your intended audience more.

ABOUT THE AUTHOR

Jason Scotts has many interests and has written many books about them. In his books, he talks about each passion how it starts, the process and how you can use it in real life situations.

Throughout the course of his career he has become familiar with the challenges that many enthusiasts have and has also found quite a number of solutions to not only solve those problems but to keep them from resurfacing in the future.

As he is aware that persons do not really have the time to be deciphering text he writes in a way that is easy for everyone to understand.

Through his text Jason helps the reader to learn new techniques or to perfect old ones. He is focused on educating and informing as the main goal to help those who are seeking answers.